Dividends

Jackson Cooper

Jackson Cooper

Copyright Page

Index

The Secret of Money That Works for You

Imagine waking up every morning and without doing anything, your bank account grows. It doesn't matter if you decide to stay in bed, travel the world, or spend the day with your family. The money keeps coming in. Not because you worked more hours or found a better-paying job, but because your money is working for you. This is the real secret to wealth: stop depending on your daily effort and build sources of income that generate money without you having to be there.

Most people spend their lives trading time for money. They get up early, go to work, stick to a schedule, and get paid at the end of the month. If they stop working, they stop earning. It's a cycle that seems impossible to break, but there is a way out: passive income. And within it, dividends and royalties are the smartest and most effective ways to make money work for you.

Dividends are payments that companies make to their shareholders as a reward for investing in them. If you buy shares of a company that pays dividends, you'll receive money from time to time without doing anything other than owning those shares. It's like owning a piece of a money-making machine that keeps running without you having to lift a finger. The more shares you own, the more money you'll receive. And the best part is that you can reinvest those payments to buy more shares, making your income grow ever larger.

Royalties, on the other hand, work in a similar way. They are payments you receive for something you created or own the rights to. They can come from books, music, patents, franchises, movies, software, or any other product that sells and continues to generate revenue without you having to be directly involved. It's the reason some authors, musicians, and entrepreneurs continue to make money years after they created something just once.

The most powerful thing about this system is that it breaks the relationship between your time and your money. While most people can only earn more by working harder, those who understand the power of passive income can earn more simply by investing better or creating assets that continue to generate money over time. This means that you don't need to be physically present to generate income. You can be on the beach, sleeping, or traveling and the money will keep flowing.

The real game of wealth isn't about working harder, it's about working smarter. It's about building a system where money flows to you consistently without your time being the limiting factor. And the key to achieving that is to start building income streams that sustain over time.

It may seem impossible at first, but the reality is that anyone with the right information and the right mindset can do it. You don't need to be a millionaire to get started, nor do you need to have advanced knowledge in finance. You just need to make the decision to stop relying solely on your job and start building assets that work for you. With every dividend investment or royalty system you put in place, you will be buying your financial freedom, getting closer to a point where money stops being a concern and becomes a tool that allows you to live the way you really want.

The secret to money working for you isn't a magic trick or an empty promise. It's a proven system that has been used by the richest people in the world to generate unlimited wealth. The only question that remains is: are you going to continue trading your time for money or are you going to start building a life where money works for you?

Types of Dividends and Royalties

When you hear the word dividends or royalties, you might think they're complicated things reserved for Wall Street investors or famous artists. But the reality is that they're simply payments you can receive on a consistent basis without having to put in extra effort. They're the key to making money without working extra hours, and best of all, there are many ways to get them. Understanding the different types of dividends and royalties will help you choose the best strategy to build a passive income stream that works for you.

Dividends are payments that companies give to their shareholders as a reward for investing in them. Not all companies pay dividends, but many do so to attract investors and maintain their trust. There are several types of dividends, and knowing them will allow you to choose which ones to invest in based on your financial goals.

The most common type is a cash dividend. It's exactly what it sounds like: the company deposits money into your account periodically, usually every quarter, just for owning its stock. This is a favorite method for those looking to live off their investments, since they can use those payments to cover expenses without selling their stock. The more shares you own, the more money you'll receive in each payment.

Another type is a stock dividend. Instead of paying you cash, the company gives you more shares, meaning your stake in the company increases without you having to invest more money. This type of dividend is ideal if you want to grow your investment over the long term, as each new share you receive will give you more dividends in the future. It's a way to take advantage of compound interest and multiply your wealth over time.

There are also special dividends, which are one-time payments that a company decides to make on specific occasions, usually when it has had a great year of profits or has sold part of its business. They are not predictable, but they can be a great unexpected bonus for investors.

Finally, there are preferred dividends, which are paid to preferred stock owners before common stock owners. While these stocks typically have less potential for price growth, they offer more stable and predictable payouts, making them attractive to those seeking consistent income.

Royalties, on the other hand, are payments you receive for something you created, own, or allow others to use. They function as a source of passive income because you continue to earn money without needing to be actively involved in the process. There are many ways to earn royalties, and each has its own advantages.

Copyright royalties are one of the most well-known. If you write a book, compose a song, create a movie, or develop software, you can get paid every time someone buys, uses, or distributes your work. Bestselling authors and musicians who have released global hits can earn millions of dollars in royalties even decades after they created their work. But you don't need to be a celebrity to benefit from this model. Many people write e-books, create online courses, or design digital images that generate passive income year after year.

Patent royalties are another powerful source of income. If you invent something and patent your creation, you can license companies to use your invention in exchange for ongoing payment. This is common in the technology and pharmaceutical industries, where innovations in software, devices, or drugs can generate millions in royalties for decades.

Another type is franchise royalties. If you create a successful business model and decide to franchise it, other people can pay to use your brand and system in exchange for a recurring fee. Restaurant chains, gyms, and convenience stores use this model to expand without having to operate each new location themselves. Franchise owners receive ongoing royalties without needing to manage each business directly.

Then there are brand licensing royalties. If you own a popular brand, you can allow other companies to use it on their products in exchange for ongoing payment. This is common in the fashion, entertainment, and sports industries. Companies like Disney generate billions in royalties simply by licensing other companies to use their characters on toys, clothing, and consumer products.

Finally, there are royalties in the oil, gas, and mining industry. If you own land rich in natural resources, you can allow companies to exploit it in exchange for a share of the profits. You don't need to do anything other than own the property to receive consistent payments.

The great thing about dividends and royalties is that you can combine them. You don't have to choose just one form of passive income. You can invest in dividend-paying stocks while building a royalty stream with a book, patent, or franchise. The more income streams you have, the more stable and predictable your cash flow will be.

In the world of business and investing, the key is not to work harder, but smarter. If you understand how dividends and royalties work, you can start building a system where money flows to you on a consistent basis. The important thing is to start as soon as possible, because time is the best ally of those looking to live off the money that works for them.

How Big Fortunes Grow with Dividends

If you look at how the world's great fortunes have been built, you'll notice a clear pattern: Most millionaires didn't make their wealth by working longer hours or relying solely on one business. Instead, they used a strategy that multiplies money without constant effort. That strategy is investing in assets that generate dividends and royalties. It's not just about buying and selling things, but about owning assets that keep generating money while they sleep.

Large fortunes grow with dividends because they allow money to be reinvested and grow exponentially over time. Imagine you buy shares of a solid company that pays dividends every quarter. Those shares generate steady payments, and instead of spending that money, you reinvest it to buy more shares. This results in your dividends being higher in the next quarter because you now own more shares that generate more payments. By repeating this process over years, your initial investment becomes a larger and larger source of income without you having to add more money out of your pocket.

This method has been used by legendary investors like Warren Buffett, who has built one of the world's largest fortunes through his focus on dividend-paying companies. Buffett doesn't just buy stocks; he looks for companies with stable businesses that pay out part of their profits to shareholders. He then reinvests those dividends to buy more stocks, allowing his wealth to grow without needing to sell his portfolio.

The secret to dividends is compound interest. Unlike a savings account, where interest is typically low and barely covers inflation, dividends can grow at a much higher rate. If a company increases its dividend every year and you keep reinvesting, your money grows at an accelerated rate. This is what allows investors to generate income over time that far exceeds what they would earn from a traditional salary.

Another clear example of how great fortunes grow with dividends is that of John D. Rockefeller, who was the richest man of his time. Rockefeller not only built his oil empire, but he was also a fan of dividends. It is said that he enjoyed receiving checks from his investments and considered dividends to be the best form of income. No matter if oil prices went up or down, he continued to receive steady payments for owning shares in profitable companies.

Today, many of the world's richest people continue to use this strategy. Large hedge funds and billionaires own stakes in companies that consistently generate dividends for them. They don't rely on just one business or one source of income, but instead build diversified portfolios that work for them.

In addition to dividends, big fortunes also grow through royalties, which work in a similar way. Companies like Disney earn billions in royalties every year simply because they own the rights to famous characters and franchises. Every time someone buys a product with Mickey Mouse's image on it, the company gets paid without doing anything extra. The same goes for tech companies that license software, book authors who generate income every time someone buys a copy, and musicians who continue to make money every time their song is played on the radio or a streaming platform.

If you want to build wealth like the great fortunes have done, the first step is to change your mindset about money. Instead of seeing money as something you must earn with your time and effort, start seeing it as a tool that can work for you. The key is to acquire assets that consistently generate dividends or royalties and reinvest those earnings into more assets.

You don't need to be a millionaire to get started. Many ordinary people have built wealth by applying this strategy with small investments that grew over time. The important thing is to start early and be consistent. Every dollar you invest in an asset that generates dividends or royalties is a soldier working for you, multiplying your money and bringing you closer to financial freedom.

Big fortunes aren't made overnight, but those who understand the power of dividends and royalties build wealth in a stable and secure way. There's no magic or luck in this, just a strategy that has been tested by the most successful investors in the world. The only question is whether you're willing to use it to your advantage.

How to Choose Companies that Pay Good Dividends

Not all dividend-paying companies are good investments. Some offer high payouts at first, but then stop being profitable, while others pay dividends consistently for decades, becoming true wealth-generating machines. Knowing how to choose companies that pay good dividends is key to building a portfolio that provides you with stable and growing passive income over time.

The first step in choosing a good dividend-paying company is to make sure its business is solid. It's not enough that a company is paying high dividends right now; you need to know if it will be able to continue paying them in the future. A company with stable and growing earnings is more reliable than one that is up and down. The best companies to invest in are usually those that operate in essential industries, such as food, energy, telecommunications, or consumer products. These companies continue to make money regardless of whether the economy is in a downturn or boom, making them safer for investors.

Another key factor is to look at the company's dividend history. If a company has paid dividends consistently for 10, 20, or even 50 years, that's a good sign. This means the company has a business model that generates enough profits to share with its investors. Even better if the company has not only paid dividends for many years, but has increased them regularly. Companies that increase their dividends year after year allow your investment to grow without needing to buy more shares. This growth is critical to protecting you against inflation and ensuring that your income increases over time.

The next point to look at is the dividend yield, which is expressed as a percentage. It is calculated by dividing the annual dividend a company pays by its share price. For example, if a company pays $5 per share per year and its stock costs $100, its dividend yield is 5 percent. A very high dividend is not always a good sign. Sometimes a company offers a high dividend because it is in trouble and its price has fallen too much. In general, a yield between 2 and 6 percent is usually safer than a company that promises to pay

10 percent or more, since too high payouts can be unsustainable.

Another important indicator is the payout ratio, which measures what percentage of a company's profits go toward paying dividends. If a company uses 80 or 90 percent of its profits to pay dividends, it can be risky, because it means it's not leaving enough money to reinvest in the business and grow. If the payout ratio is between 40 and 60 percent, on the other hand, it's a sign that the company has a healthy balance between rewarding shareholders and continuing to invest in its expansion.

You should also look at the company's debt. A company with too much debt may have trouble maintaining its dividend payments in the future, especially if the economy enters a recession. Companies with low debt and good profit margins are more likely to maintain stable and growing payments over time.

A good trick is to look at companies that are part of the so-called dividend aristocrats. These are companies that have increased their dividends for 25 years or more without interruption. Companies like Coca-Cola, Procter & Gamble and Johnson & Johnson have paid and increased their dividends for decades, demonstrating their strength and commitment to investors.

In addition to all these factors, it is essential to diversify. Don't put all your money in one company, no matter how promising it may seem. Invest in several companies in different industries to reduce risks. If one company is in trouble, the others will continue to generate income for you.

Choosing companies that pay good dividends isn't about guessing or gambling. It's about doing analysis based on hard numbers and data. By following these principles, you can build a portfolio that generates consistent and growing income without having to worry about market fluctuations. Over time, these investments will allow you to live off your dividends and achieve the financial freedom that so many people seek.

Create your First Dividend Portfolio

Building your first dividend portfolio is the first step towards financial freedom. You don't need to be an investment expert or have a lot of money to get started. The most important thing is to understand the strategy and apply it with discipline. A good dividend portfolio will allow you to generate consistent income without having to sell your shares, giving you the possibility of living off them in the future.

The first thing you need to do is define your objective. Do you want a portfolio that will provide you with immediate income or do you prefer one that will grow over time? If you are looking for immediate income, you should focus on companies that pay high and consistent dividends. If your goal is to grow your capital, it is best to invest in companies that increase their dividends every year, allowing your investment to multiply over time.

The next step is to select the right companies. Not all companies that pay dividends are good choices. You should look for solid companies with stable businesses and a proven track record of paying dividends. Ideally, you should choose companies that have paid dividends consistently for at least ten years, and even better, those that have increased them regularly. These companies demonstrate that they have a profitable business model and that they put their investors first.

Diversification is key in a dividend portfolio. Don't put all your money in one company or one industry. A well-diversified portfolio should include companies from different sectors, such as technology, consumer goods, healthcare, energy and financial services. This way, if one industry struggles, others will continue to generate income, protecting your investment over the long term.

An effective strategy is to build your portfolio with a mix of high-yield companies and dividend growth companies. High-yield companies pay high dividends now, while dividend growth companies can increase their payouts over time, allowing you to generate more income in the future.

Another important factor is dividend yield. A common mistake for beginners is to look for companies with the highest dividends without analyzing whether they are sustainable. A yield between 2 and 6 percent is a good benchmark, as companies with too high payouts may be at risk of cutting their dividends in the future.

The payout ratio is another key indicator. This number tells you what percentage of the company's profits are going towards paying dividends. A healthy payout ratio is usually between 40 and 60 percent, as it allows the company to keep reinvesting in its growth. If a company is paying out more than 80 percent of its profits in dividends, it can be a red flag, as it means it has less room to weather economic downturns or expand its business.

Once you've selected your first stocks, it's important to decide how to manage your portfolio. The best strategy to maximize your returns is to reinvest dividends into new stocks. This allows you to take advantage of the power of compound interest, making your investments grow larger and larger without needing to put up additional money.

To make dividend reinvestment easier, many companies and brokerages offer automatic reinvestment programs, known as DRIPs. With these programs, instead of receiving your dividends in cash, they are used to buy more shares of the same company without paying commissions. This accelerates the growth of your portfolio and helps you build wealth over the long term.

It's also critical to review your portfolio periodically. You don't have to do it every day, but at least once every quarter or every six months, review the performance of your investments. Check to see if companies are still paying dividends and if they have increased their payouts. If a company is reducing its dividend or is experiencing financial difficulties, consider whether it's time to sell it and look for a better option.

Dividend investing is not a get-rich-quick strategy, but rather a way to build wealth in a stable and secure manner. Over time, your dividend portfolio can become a source of passive income that allows you to live without depending on a salary.

The secret is consistency. Even if you start with small amounts, the important thing is to maintain the discipline of reinvesting dividends and keep adding new investments over time. As your portfolio grows, you will see dividend income increase significantly, bringing you ever closer to financial freedom.

Reinvestment of Dividends

Reinvesting dividends is one of the most powerful strategies for growing your wealth without additional effort. Instead of spending the money you receive from dividends, you use it to buy more stocks, which in turn generate more dividends in the future. This cycle creates a snowball effect that, over time, can turn a small investment into a significant source of income.

To understand the impact of dividend reinvestment, imagine you invest in a company that pays a 5 percent annual dividend. If you leave the dividends in your bank account, that money will just sit there without earning anything else. But if you use those dividends to buy more shares, in the next year you'll have a larger number of shares generating dividends, which means you'll receive a higher payout. As you repeat this process, growth accelerates because each new dividend generates more dividends in the future.

The secret behind this strategy is compound interest. When you reinvest your dividends, the new dividends you receive also start generating more money on their own. Over time, this compounding causes your investment to grow exponentially. That's why the most successful investors, like Warren Buffett, have built their wealth by constantly reinvesting their income instead of spending it.

The most efficient way to reinvest dividends is through automatic reinvestment programs, known as DRIPs. Many companies and brokerages offer this option, which allows dividends to be automatically used to buy more shares without you having to do anything. These programs often allow for fractional share purchases, meaning you can reinvest every penny of dividends without waiting to accumulate enough money to buy a whole share.

Another advantage of dividend reinvestment is that it helps you buy more shares automatically without worrying about the market price. When stock prices fall, dividends allow you to buy more shares at a cheaper price. When prices rise, you continue to buy, but now with the benefit of having accumulated more shares at earlier times. This method, known as cost averaging, reduces risk and allows you to profit in the long run regardless of market fluctuations.

It's important to note that dividend reinvestment is especially powerful when combined with companies that increase their dividends year after year. If you invest in companies that pay dividends and also increase them consistently, you will not only accumulate more shares over time, but each share will also generate more income in the future. This double effect accelerates the growth of your investment in an impressive way.

For example, if you buy shares of a company that pays an initial dividend of 4 percent and reinvest the dividends into new shares, after a few years you could be generating a much higher return on your initial investment. If the company also increases its dividends every year, you could end up earning 8, 10, or even 15 percent annually on your original investment without having to put up any additional money.

Another reason to reinvest dividends is that it protects you against inflation. If you simply save your dividends without reinvesting them, they will lose value over time due to the rising cost of living. But if you reinvest them in more stocks, these stocks will continue to generate increasing income, helping you maintain the purchasing power of your money.

Some investors choose to reinvest dividends in the same company that pays them, while others prefer to diversify and buy shares of other companies with that money. Both strategies can work well depending on your portfolio and your goals. Reinvesting in the same company can be beneficial if the company remains strong and profitable, while diversifying can reduce risks and allow you to take advantage of opportunities in different sectors.

The best time to stop reinvesting dividends is when you no longer need to grow your investment, but instead want to live off of passive income. At that point, instead of using dividends to buy more stocks, you can start collecting them in cash and using them to cover your expenses. If you've built a solid portfolio, dividends can become a sufficient source of income to live off of without needing to sell your stocks.

The key to success with dividend reinvestment is patience. You won't see dramatic results overnight, but if you're consistent, the effects of compound interest will become more and more evident. Over time, your initial investment can multiply several times over without you having to put up more money.

If you want to build wealth in a stable and secure way, reinvesting dividends is one of the best strategies available. It is a simple and effective way to grow your money without additional effort, taking advantage of the power of compound interest to make your investment work for you.

How to Protect Your Dividends in Times of Crisis

When the economy hits a slump, many people panic and sell their investments without thinking about the long-term consequences. However, smart investors understand that crises can be opportunities to strengthen their dividend portfolio rather than watch it fall apart. Knowing how to protect your dividends in tough times is key to keeping your passive income stable and ensuring your investment strategy continues to work no matter what happens in the world.

The first step to protecting your dividends in a crisis is to invest in solid companies from the start. Not all companies have the capacity to withstand a recession without reducing or eliminating their shareholder payouts. It is critical that your portfolio is comprised of companies with resilient business models, stable earnings, and a proven track record of paying dividends even in tough times. The best choices are often companies in essential sectors, such as food, energy, healthcare, and telecommunications, as these products and services remain in demand even in the worst economic downturns.

An important sign of a company's strength is its dividend history. If a company has paid and increased its dividends for 20, 30, or even 50 years, it has a well-run business that is capable of generating income no matter what the state of the economy. These companies, known as dividend aristocrats, are excellent choices for a crisis-resistant portfolio.

Another key point to protect your dividends is to check the payout ratio of each company you invest in. This indicator tells you what percentage of the company's profits are used to pay dividends. If the payout ratio is very high, above 80 percent, it means that the company is allocating almost all of its profits to dividends, which can be dangerous in a crisis. If the company's revenues fall during a recession, it will likely have to reduce its dividend or eliminate it altogether. A healthy payout ratio, usually between 40 and 60 percent, indicates that the company has enough room to continue paying dividends even if its revenues temporarily decline.

It's also important to diversify your portfolio. You don't want to rely on just one company or one sector to generate dividend income. If all your money is in bank stocks and the financial sector is going through a crisis, you could see cuts in your payouts. But if your portfolio is spread across different industries, some companies will continue to pay dividends even if others are struggling. Diversification is one of the most effective ways to reduce risk and ensure that you always have cash flow, no matter what happens in the market.

In times of crisis, it is advisable to have an emergency cash fund. Although dividends can provide regular income, there are times when certain companies may reduce or suspend their payments due to economic problems. Having enough cash to cover your expenses for a few months will allow you to avoid selling stocks at the worst possible time. Patience is key when investing in dividends, and an emergency fund will give you peace of mind to wait for the market to recover without affecting your investment strategy.

Another key aspect of protecting your dividends in times of crisis is to avoid selling out of fear. Many people panic when they see the value of their shares falling and end up selling at the worst possible time. If a company continues to generate income and maintains its dividend policy, there is no reason to sell just because the share price has dropped. In fact, crises can be opportunities to buy more shares at low prices and increase the amount of dividends you receive in the future.

If a company in your portfolio reduces or eliminates its dividend, it's important to analyze the situation before making any hasty decisions. Some companies make temporary cuts to protect their financial stability and then resume payments when the economy improves. In other cases, a cut can be a sign that the company is in trouble and may not recover. Evaluating the strength of the business, its debt level, and its ability to recover will help you decide whether to keep the investment or sell it and look for a better option.

It's also a good strategy to continue investing in dividends during a crisis. When stock prices fall, the dividend yield increases, meaning you can buy more shares and receive more income over the long term. Successful investors view recessions as buying opportunities rather than reasons to panic.

Protecting your dividends in times of crisis doesn't mean stopping investing or changing your strategy altogether. It means preparing yourself with a well-structured, diversified and resilient portfolio, with quality companies and solid fundamentals. If you apply these strategies, you will not only maintain your passive income in difficult times, but you will even be able to grow your portfolio when the market recovers. The key is to think long-term, stay calm and take advantage of the opportunities that crises can offer.

Create and Monetize Intellectual Property

Intellectual property is one of the most powerful and underrated ways to generate passive income. Creating something once and continuing to make money from it for years, even decades, is the dream of anyone seeking financial freedom. The best part is that anyone can do it. You don't need to be a creative genius or have an advanced degree, you just need to understand how this model works and how to take advantage of it.

Intellectual property refers to any creation of the mind that you can legally protect and monetize. This includes books, music, movies, software, digital courses, patents, trademarks, and designs. The cool thing about intellectual property is that once it's created and put on the market, it can continue to generate revenue without you having to be actively involved in the process. That's the magic of royalties.

The first step to creating and monetizing intellectual property is to identify what you can create. Not all of us are going to write the next bestseller or compose a Grammy-winning song, but there are many ways to create intellectual assets that generate consistent income. For example, writing an e-book, creating an online course, developing a mobile app, designing digital graphics, or even inventing an innovative product are all real ways to create value that can be monetized.

Let's say you decide to write a book. It doesn't have to be a literary masterpiece, it just has to solve a problem or fill a need. Nonfiction books, how-to guides, technical manuals, or even well-told fictional stories have a huge market. Once written, you can self-publish it on platforms like Amazon Kindle, where each sale will earn you a royalty. The amazing thing about this model is that the book continues to be sold every day, all over the world, without you having to do anything else after publishing it. Writing a book is an initial endeavor that can pay you for the rest of your life.

If you have specific expertise, creating an online course is another great way to generate passive income. Platforms like Udemy, Teachable, or even YouTube allow you to create content once and sell it indefinitely. People are looking to learn new skills all the time, and if your course addresses a real need, you'll continue to make money every time someone signs up. As with books, the effort is in the creation, but the rewards can last for years.

Music and digital art are also powerful forms of intellectual property. If you're a musician, every song you post on streaming platforms like Spotify or Apple Music earns you royalties every time someone listens to it. The same goes for digital art and photography. Uploading your images to platforms like Shutterstock or Adobe Stock allows you to earn money every time someone downloads your work.

For the more technically inclined, software or mobile app development is a goldmine of passive income. Creating a useful, fun, or educational app and selling it on the App Store or Google Play can generate consistent income without the need for large investments. Many successful apps were created by a single person or a small team, and generate thousands of dollars a month from downloads and in-app purchases.

Patents are another powerful form of intellectual property. If you invent something novel, you can patent your idea and license it to companies that want to make or sell your product. In return, you receive royalties on each sale without having to manufacture anything yourself. This happens a lot in industries like technology and pharmaceuticals, where innovations are highly valuable and companies are willing to pay for the right to use your creation.

Once you have your intellectual property created, the next step is to monetize it. This is where strategy comes into play. It's not enough to just create something great, you need to get it in front of the right people. This means learning how to sell your product, position it in the market, and optimize your distribution channels.

If you have a book, for example, creating a digital marketing strategy is key. Use social media, email marketing, and collaborations with other creators to generate interest. Offer promotions, create related content, and take advantage of platforms like Amazon to position your book in search results. Visibility is essential for your intellectual property to start generating consistent income.

When it comes to online courses, keeping your content high-quality and relevant is essential. Update your courses regularly, answer questions from your students, and offer additional value. This will keep your courses at the top of search results and keep attracting new students year after year.

Another important aspect is legal protection of your intellectual property. Make sure you register your copyrights, trademarks, and patents to prevent others from profiting from your work without your permission. While this may seem like a bureaucratic step, it is a necessary investment to ensure that the income from your creations is only yours.

The key to success in creating and monetizing intellectual property is to think long-term. At first, it may seem like a lot of work to create an intellectual asset, but the rewards come later. Every time someone buys your book, enrolls in your course, downloads your app, or listens to your song, you're earning money for something you did once. And as you create more assets, that income adds up, creating an ever-growing passive cash stream.

The best part is that intellectual property has no limits. You can create a single asset that generates income for years, or you can continue to create new products and expand your royalty streams. The more creations you put into the world, the more passive income you'll have.

Ultimately, creating and monetizing intellectual property doesn't just give you money, it gives you freedom. It allows you to work on your own terms, without being dependent on a fixed salary or a rigid schedule. It gives you the ability to generate income while traveling, relaxing, or spending time with your family. It's one of the smartest strategies for building wealth and living the life you truly want. And best of all, anyone can do it. You just need to get started.

Investing in Real Estate for Passive Income

Investing in real estate is one of the most proven and effective ways to generate passive income. Throughout history, many people have built their wealth by purchasing properties and renting them out to others, thereby obtaining a source of money that flows month after month without the need to exchange time for money. The most attractive thing about this type of investment is that, if done correctly, it not only provides a steady income, but also the value of the properties tends to increase over time, multiplying the profits in the long run.

To invest in real estate for passive income, the first step is to understand the different types of properties you can purchase. There are several options, including houses, apartments, commercial premises, offices, and land. Each has advantages and disadvantages, but the key is to choose one that fits your investment capacity and that is in demand in the rental market. For example, apartments in urban areas are usually easy to rent because there are many people looking for housing, while commercial premises can generate higher rents, but this depends on the performance of the business occupying them.

One of the most common strategies for generating passive income with real estate is to buy a property to rent out. The process is simple in theory: you buy a house or apartment, put it up for rent, and each month you receive money from your tenants. However, in practice, there are several factors that determine whether this investment will be profitable or become a problem. For it to truly be a source of passive income, you need to make sure you choose a property with a good location, where rental demand is high, and the rental value is sufficient to cover expenses and leave you with a profit.

Crunching the numbers before you buy is essential. It's not enough to assume that a property will be profitable just because it's in a good area. You need to consider all the associated costs, such as mortgage payments if you're buying on credit, taxes, maintenance, insurance, and possible periods when the property is vacant. A common mistake made by novice investors is to underestimate these costs and end up with a property that costs them more than it brings in. The general rule is that the monthly rent should cover all of these expenses and still leave you with a reasonable profit margin.

Another important aspect is property management. To make your income truly passive, you should not have to deal with constant maintenance issues, problematic tenants, or late payments. To do this, you can hire a property management company to take care of everything for you in exchange for a small commission on the rent. This will allow you to receive your money each month without worrying about the operational details. Although paying for management can reduce your income a little, the time and peace of mind you gain are often worth it.

An interesting strategy to increase your passive income in real estate is to use short-term rental platforms, such as Airbnb. Instead of renting out your property for long periods, you can offer it to tourists and travelers, which often generates higher income compared to a traditional rental.

However, this model requires more attention, as it involves managing reservations, cleaning the property frequently, and ensuring that the guest experience is good.

If you don't want to deal with buying and managing physical properties, another option is to invest in real estate through real estate investment trusts, known as REITs. These are companies that own and operate income-producing properties, and you can buy shares of these companies on the stock exchange. The great thing about this option is that you receive regular dividend payments without needing to buy, manage, or maintain any property. It's an easy way to get into the real estate business with a lower investment and without the complexity of owning a property.

Investing in real estate for passive income is not a get-rich-quick scheme, but it is one of the safest and most reliable strategies for building long-term wealth. Unlike other assets, a property will never lose all of its value and there will always be demand for housing and commercial space. If you choose your investments wisely and manage risks intelligently, you can ensure a steady cash flow for the rest of your life, with the possibility of expanding your portfolio and multiplying your income over time.

The key to success in real estate is planning and patience. It's not just about buying any property and waiting for the money to start rolling in. It requires research, analysis, and a strategic vision to choose the best opportunities. But once you find a profitable and well-managed investment, you can enjoy the benefits of receiving money every month without having to actively work. And that's what passive income really means.

Franchises and Businesses that Pay Royalties

Franchising and royalty-paying businesses are one of the most effective ways to generate passive income in a scalable way. These are models that allow entrepreneurs and brand creators to expand their businesses without having to be involved in every day-to-day operation. Instead of handling each unit or sale directly, they receive ongoing payments for the use of their name, product, or business model. The beauty of this system is that, once established, the money flows without the need for ongoing effort.

A franchise is a business model where one person or company (the franchisor) grants the right to another person or company (the franchisee) to operate a business using its brand, operating system, and business model in exchange for periodic payments. These payments, known as royalties, are typically calculated as a percentage of the franchisee's sales and represent ongoing revenue for the franchisor. That's why large chains like McDonald's, Subway, or 7-Eleven have grown exponentially without requiring their owners to personally manage each location.

For those looking to generate passive income, there are two main ways to take advantage of this system. The first is by creating a franchise, that is, developing a successful business that can be replicated by others. For a business to be franchisable, it must have a proven model, be profitable, and easy to replicate. Not all businesses are suitable for becoming franchises, but those that are can scale quickly and generate significant income.

The process of converting a business into a franchise involves documenting every aspect of the business's operation, from the way the operation is run to customer service processes and marketing methods. The right to use the business is then sold to entrepreneurs interested in operating the business under the same brand, in exchange for an initial payment and periodic royalty payments. The beauty of this model is that growth does not depend on the time or capital of the original owner, but on the effort of the franchisees who operate each unit.

The second way to benefit from this system is by investing in an established franchise. Instead of creating a business from scratch, you buy a franchise from a well-known brand and start operating it with the backing of a proven model. While this requires an initial investment, the advantage is that you have the support of the franchisor in terms of training, marketing and management. If chosen well, a franchise can generate passive income with relatively little effort, especially if you delegate the operation to a competent management team.

Beyond traditional franchises, there are also businesses that generate royalties without the need for a physical structure. A clear example of this is intellectual property licensing. If someone creates a character, a design or an innovative technology, they can license it to companies that want to use it in their products and receive a percentage of each sale without having to manufacture or sell anything directly. That is why comic book character creators, fashion designers and technology inventors can earn millions without having to be involved in production.

Another example of a royalty-based business is the world of music and entertainment. An artist who records a song continues to make money every time it is played on the radio, streaming platforms, or in movies and commercials. Similarly, book authors can receive royalties for every copy sold, and software creators can make money every time someone buys a license to their program.

There is also the possibility of creating subscription platforms that generate recurring revenue. Models such as Netflix, Spotify or online educational services work under this logic: customers pay a monthly amount for access to content or services, which creates a stable and predictable revenue stream. This business model is extremely attractive because it allows for scaling without the need to rely on one-off sales.

For someone who wants to generate passive income with franchises and royalties, the key is to choose a model that fits their skills and resources. If you have a strong brand and a well-defined business system, turning it into a franchise can be a profitable option. If you have valuable intellectual property, licensing it to interested companies can generate income effortlessly. And if you prefer to invest in an already proven business, buying a franchise or participating in a subscription business can be an excellent alternative.

The most important thing to understand is that royalty-based and franchise-based businesses not only make money, but they also create wealth in the long term. Unlike a traditional job where income depends on time worked, these types of models allow money to keep flowing even when you are not actively involved in the operation. And as you acquire more franchises, license more products, or build more royalty streams, passive income multiplies, allowing you to achieve financial freedom over time.

Cryptocurrencies, Staking and Decentralized Finance (DeFi)

Cryptocurrencies have revolutionized the way people can generate passive income through new strategies such as staking and decentralized finance, also known as DeFi. Unlike traditional investment methods, these systems allow anyone, without the need for large capital or banking intermediaries, to make their money work for them in a global digital ecosystem that operates twenty-four hours a day.

Staking is one of the most popular ways to generate passive income with cryptocurrencies. It works similarly to the interest a bank pays for holding money in a savings account, but in this case, instead of leaving the money in a bank, you leave cryptocurrency on a blockchain network to help validate and operate it. In exchange for this staking, you receive rewards in the form of more cryptocurrency. This is possible on networks that operate on a mechanism called proof of stake. In this model, investors lock their cryptocurrency in a smart contract and in return, the network pays them with newly generated coins, which can lead to much higher returns than a traditional savings account offers.

The advantage of staking is that it doesn't require expensive equipment or electricity, as is the case with cryptocurrency mining. You just need to purchase cryptocurrencies that support staking and deposit them into a staking-enabled wallet or delegate them to a platform that does it automatically. Some of the most popular cryptocurrencies that allow staking are Ethereum, Cardano, and Solana. Depending on the network, rewards can range from two to twenty percent per year, making it an attractive strategy for those who want to generate income without selling their assets.

However, there are risks involved in staking. One of the main ones is the volatility of the cryptocurrency price. While you can get rewards in the form of more coins, if the value of the cryptocurrency drops dramatically, the gain in tokens may not compensate for the loss in asset value. That's why it's important to choose solid projects and diversify your investments rather than betting everything on a single cryptocurrency.

Beyond staking, decentralized finance has opened up a new era of opportunities to generate passive income without relying on banks or traditional financial institutions. DeFi is an ecosystem of applications that allows lending, interest earning, asset trading, and many other financial activities without intermediaries. Everything is executed through smart contracts, which are automated programs that operate on blockchains like Ethereum.

One of the most popular ways to earn passive income in DeFi is through lending protocols. In these systems, investors can deposit their cryptocurrencies on a platform that then lends these funds to other users in exchange for interest. Unlike banks, where interest rates are typically low, in DeFi rates can be significantly higher, depending on the supply and demand of each asset. Additionally, loans are secured with cryptocurrency collateral, which reduces the risk of default.

Another common strategy in the DeFi world is liquidity provision. Many decentralized platforms allow users to deposit their cryptocurrencies into liquidity pools, which are used to facilitate the exchange of assets on decentralized markets. In return, liquidity providers receive a portion of the fees generated by these exchanges, which can translate into steady income if trading volume is high. However, this method comes with risks such as impermanent loss, which occurs when the prices of the deposited assets change significantly, affecting the total value of the investment.

The opportunities in cryptocurrencies, staking, and DeFi are huge, but they also require education and caution. Because this is a new and constantly evolving ecosystem, there are risks such as falling asset values, bugs in smart contracts, or even fraud in malicious projects. Therefore, before investing in any strategy, it is essential to thoroughly research, diversify investments, and use recognized platforms with high levels of security.

The most attractive thing about this new financial system is that it puts control in the hands of investors and offers opportunities to generate passive income without the restrictions of the traditional banking world. For those willing to learn and manage risks intelligently, cryptocurrencies and decentralized finance represent a new frontier of financial freedom and long-term wealth generation.

Financial Planning to Live Off Dividends

Living off dividends is the dream of many investors. The idea of receiving a constant income without having to work actively sounds like the perfect plan to achieve financial freedom. However, for this to become a reality, well-structured financial planning is essential. It is not just about investing in companies that pay dividends, but doing so in a strategic way that guarantees sufficient income to cover all expenses for life without the initial capital running out.

The first step in financial planning for living off of dividends is to calculate how much money is needed to maintain the desired lifestyle. This involves doing a detailed analysis of monthly and annual expenses, including housing, food, transportation, insurance, entertainment, and any other recurring expenses. It is important to be realistic and consider even unexpected or emergency expenses, as the goal is to live off this income without relying on other sources.

Once the amount needed to cover expenses has been determined, the next step is to calculate how much capital is required to invest to generate that passive income. To do this, the average yield of dividend-paying stocks must be considered. If, for example, the portfolio generates a four percent annual dividend yield and it takes fifty thousand dollars a year to live, then an investment portfolio of at least one million two hundred and fifty thousand dollars would be required.

This calculation is a starting point, but the key is to structure the portfolio in a way that ensures stability and growth over time. It's not just about finding the companies with the highest dividends, but looking for solid companies that can maintain and increase their payouts in the future. Companies with a history of consistent dividend growth are ideal, as this means that over time the passive income will increase without the need to reinvest more money.

Another crucial aspect in planning is diversification. Relying on just one sector or a few companies can be risky, as any crisis or dividend cut could seriously affect income. To avoid this, it is advisable to build a diversified portfolio with companies from different sectors such as technology, healthcare, real estate, consumer goods and energy. It is also useful to consider dividend investment funds or REITs, which are real estate investment trusts that distribute income regularly.

The dividend reinvestment strategy plays an important role in accumulating wealth before reaching the point where you can live entirely off passive income. Until you need the dividend money, it is best to reinvest it to buy more stocks and take advantage of compound interest. Over time, this multiplier effect can make a portfolio grow significantly without the need to add more capital.

When you finally reach the level of investment necessary to live off dividends, the next phase of planning is managing the withdrawal of income. Some people choose to withdraw only the dividends and leave the principal intact, while others combine dividends with the occasional sale of stock to supplement income. It is important to consider factors such as inflation, taxes, and the possibility of adjustments to dividend payments.

In terms of taxes, knowing the dividend tax regulations in the country where you reside is essential. In some places, dividends have reduced tax rates compared to other income, while in others they may be subject to high taxes. Planning with a financial advisor can help minimize the tax burden and maximize net income.

It is also advisable to have an emergency fund in cash or liquid investments to cover any unforeseen events without having to sell shares in times of market crisis. This avoids having to sell assets at low prices and allows you to maintain financial stability even in times of uncertainty.

The key to living off dividends is not just investing, but doing so strategically and with a long-term mindset. Building a solid, diversified portfolio with sustainable growth over time ensures that passive income is reliable and sufficient to cover the cost of living. With patience, discipline and planning, anyone can reach a point where money works for them and not the other way around.

How to Avoid the Most Common Dividend Mistakes

Dividend investing may seem like a sure path to financial freedom, but there are many mistakes that investors make that can cause their strategy to fail. Some of these mistakes are the result of a lack of knowledge, while others occur because they want to get quick results without properly evaluating the risks. Avoiding them is key to building a solid and reliable portfolio that generates stable passive income over the long term.

One of the most common mistakes is investing in stocks just because they pay a very high dividend. Many people see a dividend yield of eight, ten, or even fifteen percent and think they've found a gold mine. However, a dividend that is too high is often a warning sign. It can indicate that the company is in financial trouble and, in order to attract investors, is maintaining an unsustainable dividend that will eventually be cut. Instead of being carried away by the dividend percentage alone, it is better to look at the company's financial health and its actual ability to continue paying those dividends in the future.

Another common mistake is not diversifying. Many investors fall into the trap of putting most of their money in a few high-dividend companies, without considering that any problems in one of them can seriously affect their income. To avoid this risk, it is essential to build a diversified portfolio with companies from different sectors, geographies and sizes. Including dividend mutual funds or real estate investment trusts can help reduce exposure to any problems specific to a single company or industry.

Some investors also make the mistake of not reinvesting their dividends. If the goal is to build wealth, reinvesting dividends is one of the most powerful strategies thanks to the effect of compound interest. Every time dividends are reinvested, more shares are purchased, which in turn generates more dividends in the future. Over time, this cycle creates exponential growth in the portfolio. Failing to take advantage of this tool can make the process of wealth accumulation much slower than it could be.

Another common mistake is ignoring dividend growth. Not all companies maintain or increase their dividends over time. Some companies may look attractive at first because they pay a high dividend, but if they don't have a history of growth, the value of that payment will be eroded by inflation over the years. It's best to invest in companies that not only pay dividends, but consistently increase them. Companies with decades of dividend increases are often more stable and reliable over the long term.

Some investors also underestimate the importance of taxes. Depending on the country, dividends may be subject to different tax rates, and failure to plan properly can significantly reduce net income. It is advisable to be aware of the tax rules and, if possible, invest in tax-advantaged accounts that allow you to minimize taxes on dividends.

One big mistake many people make is selling dividend stocks too quickly. It can be tempting to sell a stock when the price rises to take a quick profit, but if the company continues to pay and increase its dividends, selling it can mean losing valuable passive income in the future. Dividend investing is a long-term strategy, and success depends on patience and consistency.

On the other hand, some investors do the opposite and hold on to companies that have stopped being profitable just because they paid good dividends in the past. When a company reduces or eliminates its dividend, it is a sign that something is not right. In these cases, it is best to analyze the situation objectively and decide whether it is really worth continuing to invest in the company. Sometimes, selling and moving the money to a more stable company is the best decision.

Another mistake that can seriously affect a dividend investing strategy is not having an emergency fund. Although dividends can be a reliable source of income, there is always the risk that a recession or market crisis will force companies to reduce or suspend their payouts. If an investor relies solely on dividends and does not have a backup fund, they may find themselves in a difficult situation if payouts suddenly decrease.

Having an emergency fund in cash or liquid assets helps maintain financial stability in times of uncertainty.

Finally, one of the most costly mistakes is not having a clear plan. Many investors buy dividend stocks without a defined strategy, hoping that time will do the work for them. However, it is essential to set clear financial goals, review the portfolio periodically and make adjustments as necessary. A good plan includes selecting quality companies, appropriate diversification, reinvesting dividends and managing risks.

Dividend investing is one of the most effective strategies for generating passive income and building wealth, but it only works well if you avoid these mistakes. With a long-term mindset, proper planning, and constant portfolio review, anyone can harness the power of dividends to achieve financial independence.

How to Scale and Expand Your Passive Income Strategy

Building a passive income strategy based on dividends and royalties is a great first step toward financial freedom, but true growth happens when you learn how to scale and expand that strategy. Many people start by investing small amounts and see their passive income grow over time, but if you want to speed up the process and maximize your profits, you need to implement specific strategies that will allow you to increase your profits without unnecessarily increasing your risk.

The first step to scaling a passive income strategy is to systematically increase the amount of capital invested. Many people start with a modest amount, but to really scale the strategy you need to find ways to consistently bring in more capital. This can be done by increasing savings earmarked for investments, finding new sources of income to reinvest, or even using generated passive income to purchase more assets. The key is to grow the portfolio without needing to rely solely on active work.

Automatic reinvestment of passive income is another key pillar of scaling the strategy. If the dividends and royalties generated are not spent, but instead reinvested to buy more productive assets, the effect of compound interest begins to play a crucial role. Over time, this exponential growth can make a relatively small initial investment turn into a significant source of income. Scheduling the reinvestment of dividends into additional stocks or earmarking royalties for new investments ensures that the money continues to work and multiply without interruption.

Another key approach to expansion is to diversify passive income sources. Relying exclusively on a single type of asset, such as dividend stocks, can be risky if the market enters a downturn. To mitigate that risk, other passive income sources such as real estate, royalties, franchises, or cryptocurrency investments can be explored. Diversification not only protects the portfolio in times of uncertainty, but also opens up new growth opportunities.

Well-used financial leverage can also accelerate expansion. This means using borrowed capital wisely to acquire productive assets that generate passive income above the cost of financing. In real estate, for example, mortgage financing can be used to purchase rental properties without having to pay the full price up front. In stock investing, some investors cautiously use margin strategies to expand their portfolio without completely depleting their capital. However, leverage must be managed responsibly, as excessive or imprudent use can significantly increase risk.

In addition to investing more capital and diversifying, it is important to optimize the profitability of existing assets. This means looking for stocks of companies that regularly increase their dividends, renegotiating royalty contracts to obtain better terms, or improving the management of rental properties to increase their profitability. Continuous optimization of passive income is a key strategy to maximize returns without the need to increase risks.

Another effective way to scale a passive income strategy is to leverage automation. Technology makes it possible to automate dividend investing through reinvestment plans, use rental management platforms to minimize operational burden on real estate, or even implement online passive income strategies without the need for constant oversight. The more automated the strategy is, the easier it is to scale without the investor having to spend too much time on day-to-day management.

It is also advisable to use passive income to acquire assets that generate even more income. Instead of spending dividends or royalties on consumer expenses, they can be used to buy semi-automated businesses, fund royalty-paying startups, or acquire rental properties. This aggressive reinvestment mindset accelerates portfolio growth and significantly shortens the time needed to achieve financial independence.

An advanced strategy for scaling is to build an ecosystem of interconnected passive income. For example, someone who generates book royalties can reinvest that income into dividend stocks, and in turn use those dividends to buy real estate. In this way, each income stream feeds the others, creating a self-sustaining financial system that grows exponentially over time.

As the portfolio grows, it is also important to implement tax strategies to protect passive income. Depending on the investment structure, tools such as tax-advantaged trusts, companies, or mutual funds can be used to minimize the tax burden and maximize net returns. A good financial advisor can help design a strategy that optimizes the tax structure without affecting liquidity or financial security.

Finally, the most important aspect of scaling a passive income strategy is the growth mindset. Many people settle for a level of passive income that covers the basics, but those who truly achieve financial independence are those who constantly seek out new investment, optimization, and expansion opportunities. The key is to never stop learning, adapt to market changes, and look for innovative ways to make money work even more efficiently.

Scaling and expanding a passive income strategy isn't just about investing more money, it's about doing so intelligently and strategically. Growing capital, diversifying, optimizing assets, using leverage cautiously, and reinvesting income are all critical elements to accelerating the path to financial freedom. With discipline, long-term vision, and consistent execution, anyone can turn a modest source of passive income into a solid system that continuously generates wealth.

Live off Dividends and Royalties

Living off dividends and royalties is not an unattainable dream reserved only for big investors or entrepreneurs with inherited fortunes. It is a reality that anyone with discipline, strategy and a long-term vision can build. The key is to develop a system that generates constant income without the need to exchange time for money. Unlike traditional work, where you receive a salary in exchange for hours of effort, dividends and royalties allow money to flow regardless of whether you work or not.

To make a living off of dividends and royalties, it is essential to build a solid financial foundation. It is not about simply receiving some occasional payments, but about generating enough passive income to cover all essential expenses and, eventually, enjoy a life without financial worries. Most people who achieve this goal do not do it overnight. It is a process that requires time, patience and a well-defined strategy.

The first step is to determine how much money you need to live comfortably without relying on a job. This involves making a detailed calculation of your monthly expenses, including housing, food, transportation, health, entertainment, and any other recurring expenses. Once you have a clear figure, you need to determine how much passive income you need to generate to cover those costs. If, for example, a person needs $3,000 a month to live, you'll need to make sure your investments and royalties generate that amount in a stable and predictable way.

Dividends are a key source of passive income to achieve this goal. Companies that consistently pay dividends can become the backbone of a portfolio designed for financial independence. The strategy is to select stocks from companies with a solid history of paying and increasing dividends, reinvest them in more stocks while building the portfolio, and, once the income goal is reached, begin living off those payments. The advantage of dividends is that they come from companies that continue to operate and generate profits, making the payouts relatively stable and, in many cases, increasing over time.

Royalties are another avenue for building long-lasting passive income. Unlike dividends, which come from investments in companies, royalties arise from the creation or ownership of intellectual or business assets. This includes books, music, patents, software licenses, franchises, and even digital content. Many people have managed to live solely off of royalties, creating products once and receiving payments for years without needing to actively work on them.

The ideal balance is to diversify passive income sources. Relying solely on dividends or royalties can be risky if one source of income is affected by market changes. Those who live off passive income often combine dividend investments with royalty-generating assets and, in some cases, rental real estate. This combination helps protect against economic downturns and maintain long-term financial stability.

One of the most common mistakes is to start relying on passive income too early. Many people get excited when they start receiving dividend and royalty payments and decide to quit their job without making sure the income is sustainable. To avoid this, it is recommended to keep reinvesting all passive income until it reaches a high enough level to cover expenses with a margin of safety. It is best to wait a few more years and make sure the system is well established before making a full transition to living off of passive income alone.

Another key factor is tax efficiency. It's not enough to receive passive income; you also have to make sure that taxes don't drastically reduce your earnings. Depending on the country, there are legal strategies to minimize your tax burden, such as investing in tax-advantaged accounts, structuring businesses efficiently, or diversifying income across different jurisdictions. Having a financial advisor who understands tax optimization can make a big difference in how much money you have available to live on.

The lifestyle of a person who lives off dividends and royalties is also important. Many times, those who achieve financial independence find that they do not need to spend as much money as they thought. Without the pressure of a job, expenses can be significantly reduced by moving to a cheaper location, avoiding unnecessary expenses, or simply adopting a simpler, more relaxed lifestyle. True wealth is not just about how much money you have, but the freedom to decide how to live without being tied to a job or the need to constantly generate more income.

For many people, living off passive income doesn't mean stopping working altogether, but rather having the option to only do projects they truly enjoy. Some continue to create content, invest in new businesses, or develop innovative ideas because they are passionate about it. The big difference is that they no longer do it out of necessity, but by choice. That's the true essence of financial independence.

Building a passive income system based on dividends and royalties not only provides financial stability, but also allows you to design a life without financial stress. It is not about getting rich overnight, but about building a solid foundation that allows money to come in automatically and consistently. With a well-structured strategy, discipline, and patience, anyone can achieve this goal and live a life where money works for them instead of them working for money.

www.ingramcontent.com/pod-product-compliance
Lightning Source LLC
LaVergne TN
LVHW090424210926
848480LV00002B/676
* 9 7 9 8 2 3 0 6 2 1 4 0 9 *